STAY CLOSE WITH BOOKS
MAGERS & QUINN
BOOKSELLERS
MINNEAPOLIS
AGERSANDQUINN.COM

CPSIA information can be obtained
at www.ICGtesting.com
Printed in the USA
LVHW042211280720
661796LV00002B/480

9 781097 94116